I0274250

# Beneath the Veil
# She Speaks

**~Selected Poems By~**

**D. J. Williby**

Beneath the Veil She Speaks



ISBN: 978-0-692-70291-8

Library of Congress Control Number: 2016904566

Softcover: First Edition / First Printing



Debra June Williby-Walker

12018 Ingleside Road

Oakvale, WV 24739

**Photo and Art Credits:**

D. J. Williby pgs. 13, 16, 20, 22, 34, 42, 45, 50, 56, 57, 82, 83

Moriah Walker pg. 52

Ellen Chychul pgs. 55, 73

Delbert Whitlow pg. 19

Rita McCoy Rodriguez pg. 24

Lisa Rae Ring pgs. 28, 30, 44, 54

Lovietta Sebastian pg. 33

LaTisha Walker pg. 40

Barbara J. Houghton pgs. 14, 53, 74, Cover

Sheila Burke pgs. 39, 61

Rae Manning pgs. 68, 80

Braydin Michael-Andrew Walker pg. 84

A. M. Toussaint pgs. 18, 60, 76

Amber Dunford pg. 46

Sheila Long-Dicey pgs. 62, 64

David Lester pg. 70

Tressie Hamm pg. 66

Marcus Walker pg. 78

Sharon Williby pg. 26

Teresa Byars pgs. 36, 58

Savana Mills pgs. 38, 72

Eddie Redden pg. 48

Taylor K. Hamm- BC Photo

Additional copies of this book may be purchased at Createspace.com/6116246, Amazon.com or Amazon.co.uk

## Table of Contents

**Unseen Tribulations**

## Dedication

For my dad, Larry and my mother, Ginger: Thanks for my practical side, Daddy! I can grow a mean garden too! Oh, and for the education of 'win at any cost!' I never back down! From you, I acquired my love of nature. As for you mother, you are that still small voice whispering in my ear, "This is the way, walk in it!" Many thanks mother for instilling the love of reading and poetry in my life at a small age. If my verse helps one soul, it will be worthwhile.

For my brother, Danny and my sister, Tressie: I can still go from zero to full-blown crazy in a matter of seconds! Nothing has changed! I would fight a 'circle' saw over y'all! Yeah, I know, it is a circular saw grammar police! Ain't a thing wrong with my dialect and cuttin' words short! I'm from the hills of West Virginia! We know the difference! You just do not know that we know!

For my son, Marcus and my daughter, Moriah: You two have put me through more hell and changes than I care to count but my heart bleeds love for you both! I don't wanta hear a peep outta y'all! Don't get it twisted folks! "We fight together!" Also for my second son, David: Love you with all my heart too! No Worries! Elliot still resides in my refrigerator! 15 Years Now!

For my nieces and nephews, Rae, Taylor, Jared, Zachary, Marshall, and Benjamin: Y'all once had a 'goat' of a time with none other than myself! "Got Goat?" A special shout out to Taylor that always tries to feed me and includes me in her daring adventures! Zip-lining anyone?

For my grandchildren, Layla Boo, Brady, Zelly, Ayce, and Kee-Jay: You have brought much joy and love into my life. Plus, all kinds of racket! Remember, Marmee is always right no matter what your parents may say! It is okay to color outside the lines no matter who tells you otherwise!

For the thorn in my side, Charles: I doubt I become rich! As Stevie Nicks and Dave Stewart sings, "We are cheaper than free!"

For my sidekick and partner in crime, Anita Dunn: Thanks for helping me throughout this process and please stop singing, 'Daddy's Home' and stop climbing to help me! You were black and blue from that fall! Love you much, sista! Oh yeah, How 'bout a trip back to the Corner Shop in Bramwell to eat? Soon I hope so we can sing on stage with the Mo Jo Sisters again!

For my kindred spirits that suffer with a mental illness and major depression: You understand my madness and musings. "If you are depressed, do not worry about pressing any number. No one will answer you anyway!" What an awesome Mental Health Hotline Ringtone I have on my phone!

For all West Virginians and especially Oakvalians: We 'ain't plumb dumb' like most people think!

Not for those who misunderstand and mock my being: Backatcha! Get over it! Remember? "Watch me!" Here it is! Ha!

## Inner-Circle Reviews

As a friend of the author for many moons, we have shared many laughs, thoughts, ideas, feelings, and good times. I am honored to have been involved in seeing this book come to life. This journey is one that I will never forget, for I have enjoyed chatting via the internet, the long nighttime conversations, editing, numerous phone calls, country outings, great food, and awesome music as well. My! My! My! The hours!

Not only have I been a part of this entire process I have been amazed at how the author self-meditates through her writings, which have touched my life in many ways. As you read this collection of poetry, I know you will develop the same feelings that I have experienced with this particular author. There is no greater gift than sharing the journey with others.

~A. M. Toussaint~

I remember making Deb'z acquaintance on Facebook around September of 2014. We both had a couple of things in common and right off the bat, I thought, whoa, she is trying to collect 1000 items of non-perishable food to help folks. I happened to be in a position to help a little bit that day and it was just so cool because it sorta ended up snowballing. Well, without running on too much, I could see that God was working.

As I conversed with Deb'z one night, I leapt for joy the moment she said she was a poet. I was a songwriter with a block that day. She trusted me enough to allow me to attempt to put some of her verse to song. Two of them evolved. ('Release Me' based on her poem 'The Flow' and 'Refugee' based on her poem 'I am a Refugee'). However, Deb'z already knows this.

The secret that I have never revealed until now is I was going to quit music the night I met her. I find it fascinating that the first poem she gave me got me through that tough spot. You see, I was stuck when God sent her my way. Deb'z is not just my muse, she has been my therapist, my counselor, my teacher, and she is part of an incredibly small group of people that I know I can trust on every level. The friendship is even more special when it is recognized that a bond can exist when two people have never been closer than 1500 miles and not had the opportunity to sit as friends. However, it exists and it is such a rare thing when trust is hard to come by in today's world where most folks do not know their neighbor.

~Eric Reusch~

I had the privilege of reading 'Beneath the Veil She Speaks' pre-book. I was transcended into life through Deb'z writings that drew me in immediately. Her verse touched my heart and opened my eyes to thoughts that filled me, as I become one with her. As I read how she felt in both joy and pain, and ultimately finding tranquility, I felt kinship. The simplistic pleasure I felt as I read her work, made me want to read it over and over as I search and discover new truths each time I read.

~Sharon Williby~

She proves once again that she can do anything she makes up her mind to do. Out of the 35+ years that I have known the author, she has always done amazing things. Debbee is a free spirited old soul with a kind heart. She is well-known for always helping others before helping herself. Writing this poetry collection was to do just that! Her reasoning was not self-centered. It was in hopes of helping others who may relate or share the same struggles and triumphs.

I am sure after reading this poetry collection, it will touch each and everyone's hearts as it has mine. Her poetry describes how she learned to live with a mental illness and depression, and the section on how she connects to nature is very insightful. To venture into the darkness and come out 'Into the Light' as a spiritual being is beyond all reasoning! She speaks to us all and gives us a glimpse of her inner-self hidden for years.

~Charles David Walker Jr.~

**Acknowledgements**

Behind my quest to compile this collection of verse, I had a team of kindred spirits that helped me through the process! Many thanks to those who walked this journey with me and may God shower you all with much joy, laughter, and happiness!

Much gratitude to my dear friends, Delbert Whitlow, A. M. Toussaint, Jason Parks, Luis Lozano, and Barbara J. Houghton for all the time spent helping me edit photos, as you all know I am not Word and computer savvy! To you may the blessings of the Most High grant you your wishes and dreams as you helped me achieve mine. Without you, this would not have been possible.

It is nice to know I have four family members that believe in me and appreciate my writings. Thanks to you, Mother and Brady for reading and listening to my poetry repeatedly throughout the entire process. Also a shout out to my Aunt June that I am named after and have much in common with physically and mentally! You get me when no one else does! Known as your 'Namesake' we both know not one person that wants to experience the wrath of June and definitely not two Junes at once! (Smiles). To you Angela Williby-Emmerson, A huge thanks for always believing in me, reading my verse and the nighttime phone calls! If the world ever heard those conversations, we would be locked in a padded room! (Wink, Wink). Great minds, think alike!

Thanks to my Mother, Ginger Williby, Jacqueline Rucker, and Sharon Williby for proofreading and taking the time to read my verse thoroughly. No one else I asked would enter that arena!

A huge thanks to several artistic folks who valued my poetry enough to contribute their own art for my collection. Eddie Redden, Rae Manning, Brady Walker, Barbara J. Houghton, and Savana Mills may you always use your talent for the glory of God and may your creative abilities continue to flow. Gifted you are!

Thanks to my greatest fan base Ellen Chychul, Sheila Long and Sheila Burke for encouragement and support! Many times you listened to me rant in messages and responded to my rants on Facebook when I was about to give up! You ladies kept me afloat and focused!

Thanks to my Facebook friends that read and commented their thoughts on my poetry I shared. Especially, Michael Sabastian, Rina Human, Sally Keen, Marcella Dennison, Lisa Ring, Charlotte Pruett, Carly Mills, Nola Snider, John Burgess, Kathy Easley, Ursula Candasamy, Fred Woodby, Twig Dee, Joann Mitchell, Barbara Justine King, Cynthia D. Repass, and Carolyn Jones.

Much love and thanks goes out to Cliff Nash, author of 'Carol and Me' for his insight into the publishing world and for his constructive criticism and suggesting photographs with my poems! Thanks Cliff! It worked out brilliantly. As for your gospel/jazz album 'Look Toward Jordan' it has pulled me from the pits of despair on many sleepless nights. Musically, you have been my inspiration.

To you Peter Shoesmith, I am grateful for the time you took to read my verse and for all the feedback and constructive criticism. From you I found much encouragement and help during my battles with depression by watching your short video/film for 'Mind.' Thank you so much for taking the time to share it with me! I visit it often!

Steven David, Your constructive criticism helped me much and I will forever be at your mercy! You lifted my spirits when I was at my lowest. Not sure you knew, but you did! I may very well be your long lost sister as you asked! (Smiles).

Barbara Justine King, Thanks a bunch for the many outings to Starbucks in Princeton, West Virginia! Having access to WiFi is a must when correcting and uploading files for publication. Without your help, this would have never happened!

Ursula Candasamy my dear kindred spirit across the pond, thanks for the encouragement and feedback on my verse. It means so much. It has been my pleasure working with you in our charity efforts in South Africa and West Virginia. In the spirit of Ubuntu, the world's humanity is our humanity. Mwah!

Cameron Pennington, I love you! You are one of the friends that I can count on at any time if I need you. Thanks for all the chats and encouragement you gave me while I was about to give up! You Rock! Please schedule me in your calendar for an appointment. My hair "looks a hot mess" as you often tell me! Haha

Thanks to Charles D. Walker Jr. for proofreading and finding a few errors for me the day of submission. Shew! Weee! Talk about last minute edits! I appreciate that very much!

Eric Reusch and A.M. Toussaint, Not enough thanks can explain my gratitude. I feel like I owe you both my left kidney! Not that I want either of you to need one but mine will be available if needed! You two traveled this journey with me from beginning to end! Whoa! What a time we had in the wee hours of the night! May you always be fruitful in your gift of giving not only through charity work for others in need but also your ability to help others achieve their dreams! Thanks for seeing my dream birthed into reality!

Last but not least, to the muse of my making, Anthony (aeteni/antony) without your awakenings I would have never put pen to paper. Much love to you my friend!

**In Jesus' Name**

During the process of me compiling my poetry collection, I had the support of my aunt Beverly June Redden. She always took the time to read and support my endeavor and she most certainly understood my verse. On December 1, 2015 my aunt, June entered Paradise to be with Jesus. Known for our tempers, mental illnesses, depression, and firm belief in Jesus Christ, we were cut from the same mold. As many of our Facebook friends know, June always signed off "In Jesus' Name" and with a saddened joyous heart, I have done the same here in her honor.

## Introduction

After years of staying to myself and using writing as a tool to express myself, I finally shared some of my writings with a few kindred spirits and was encouraged to compile some of them in this poetry collection. It reveals where I have been, others I have met and some spirits by way of my musings. Through my experiences and trials, I speak truth as to what it is like to live with racing thoughts and troubled experiences. My soul purpose is to connect with readers of a similar nature and kindle a relationship that lets others know, they are not alone.

In section three, 'Unseen Tribulations' my struggles with a mental illness, depression, and other life experiences that have often brought me to my knees are revealed. At this stage in my life, I have learned to embrace my flaws and fallacies. To accept just part of who I am would not yield truth. Therefore, I consider all aspects as the making of the person I have become. Artwork and photographs compliment my poems to give a visual interpretation to help guide you in your quest to read my verse.

In section two, 'Channeled through Nature' you will view many different avenues of nature and see how my love of the outdoors helps me deal with the chaotic world around me. They most certainly deal with how I handle heartaches, and experiences. In this section, you will discover, I am one with nature. The connection has saved me from falling deep into depression and a realm filled with misery. To God I give all the glory as I see Him in all the beauty bestowed upon us and these wonders have saved me and gave me hope when all else has failed.

In section one, 'Into the Light' you will see where I evolved into my spirituality, my fascination with what most deem non-existent but as for me, I find comfort in folklore, and the supernatural. My imagination that runs amuck and for those who truly believe will find comfort in the fancies of the unreal. They offer hope. I also try to provide comfort to loved ones of those who have moved on into the afterlife. To provide a wee bit of comfort and peace to loved ones left behind with my verse, gives me purpose.

As with section three, sections one and two are complimented by artwork and photography as a guide into the senses. The interpretation of my verse is open to the reader as no two people see the world in the same light. The artwork and photographs are the mere interpretations from kindred spirits and family and some are those in which I incorporated. As someone who is visual by nature, I felt the need to display the creativity of those within my small circle. This collection is very personal and the need to cover all areas of my being was essential. It was necessary to include the work of those I connect with in person and those I have connected with via social media. They play a role in my existence.

As one who has suffered with a mental illness and major depression since a teen, it was only in my latter years that I began to talk openly about my plights. Often times we tend to hide who we are and not 'rock the boat' of those in which society deems normal.

Through much personal growth and searching deep within, I have found peace. It is my hope that my verse reaches those who also struggle with mental illnesses or depression and if it helps just one soul, I have succeeded in my endeavor. Poetry is an art form to be shared and this collection is an avenue for me to draw back the veil I feel comfortable behind if only for a brief moment to speak. Those walls I have built within, that veil that covers me, and the distance I keep is part of who I am. I have learned to accept who I am and coming to the realization that having a mental illness and suffering with major depression is not a curse but a part of me that brings out the best of my creativity.

It is my hope that this brief introduction and explanation of each section gives you a glimpse of who I am and how important it was for me to use the artwork, and photographs of those who understand what it is like to be eccentric, different, and most definitely a 'crazmo' as some have often voiced. At this point in my life, I accept all those descriptions of me as compliments as I have learned to embrace my whole being. It is those who have been through the same struggles that understand and keeps me going. My heart is the canvas upon which kindred spirits paint their masterpieces. To them I dedicate my life. For without them, my existence would cease.

In essence, I have never been one to discuss my personal, chaotic life nor have I been one to reveal just who I am. I have always found myself building up a wall or hiding my true self and feelings. Through reading and writing poetry, I have learned to dance to the song of my enemies and slip away quietly to create a harmony of my own.

## Poetry Style and Form

Just a note to address the poetry form in my collection, I have never been one to conform or adhere to rules so most of the poems in this collection are in free verse. However, I have included my stab at an English sonnet, a Persian form of poetry that originated in Arabic called a Ghazal, several acrostics poems and Haiku poetry fused into artwork and photographs. To those who are strict in their thinking and reading of poems that follow a specific form, I apologize. I view poetry as open to the writer and standard rules do not apply in my world. In regards to my view on how to read them, I leave that entirely up to the reader.

Forever in His Grace,

Deb'z

*"Poetry is for dreamers that take a temporary expedition into the very soul of all things living." ~Deb'z~*

Williby-Walker, Debra. 'Into the Light.' Williby Farm. Photograph. 2015.

Personal Collection. Oakvale, West Virginia.

Houghton, Barbara J. 'The Awakener.' Pencil Sketch enhanced with Graphic Art. 2015.

Personal Collection. Mercer County, West Virginia.

**The Awakener**

a muse comes to me in the night
...softly whispers an invitational song of delight
the noble deed does not go unnoticed
as i contemplate lyrical perfection
i am the laureate that trembles
...the climax of the honor soothes my soul

Williby-Walker, Debra. 'Canterbury Cathedral.' Canterbury, Kent, United Kingdom.

Photograph. 1998. Personal Collection. Oakvale, West Virginia.

## The Reading

the sages and prophets failed an interpretation of a dream
and the spirit of the one who weeps yearns for comfort
as no response is given

when the world fell into a slumber of sleep
an oracle called to the one wise to hear
a divine revelation revealed as the petitioner arises

the natural and spiritual world meets as the desire
for knowledge is discerned and visible
cloaked by a mist of droplets the messenger dispatches the winds

a calming peace circulated and a burden is lifted
all is well with the weeper as clarification is sealed
the divination of the oracle magically appeared

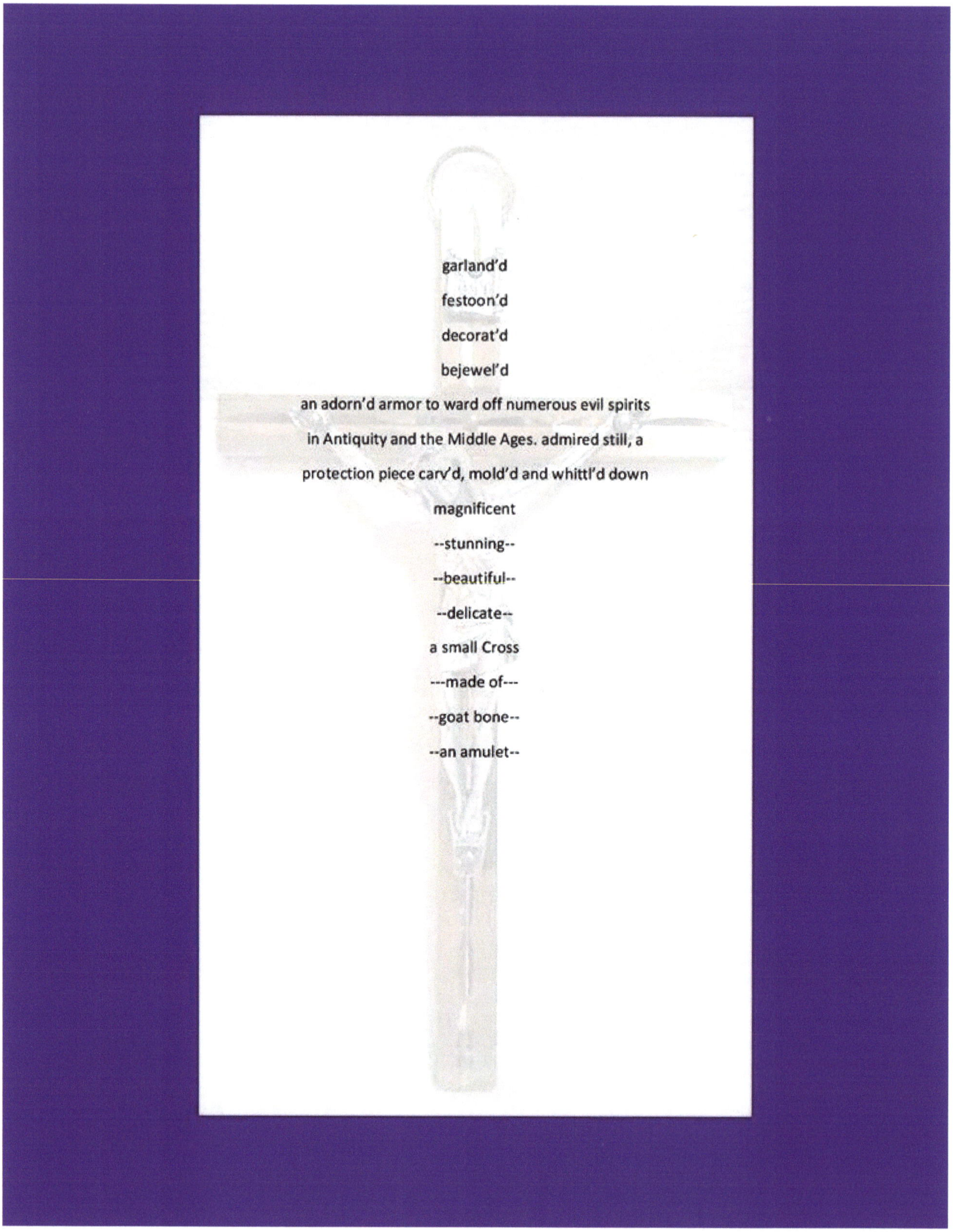


Toussaint, A. M. 'Le Tout-Puissant.' Photograph. 2015. Personal Collection, Princeton, West Virginia.

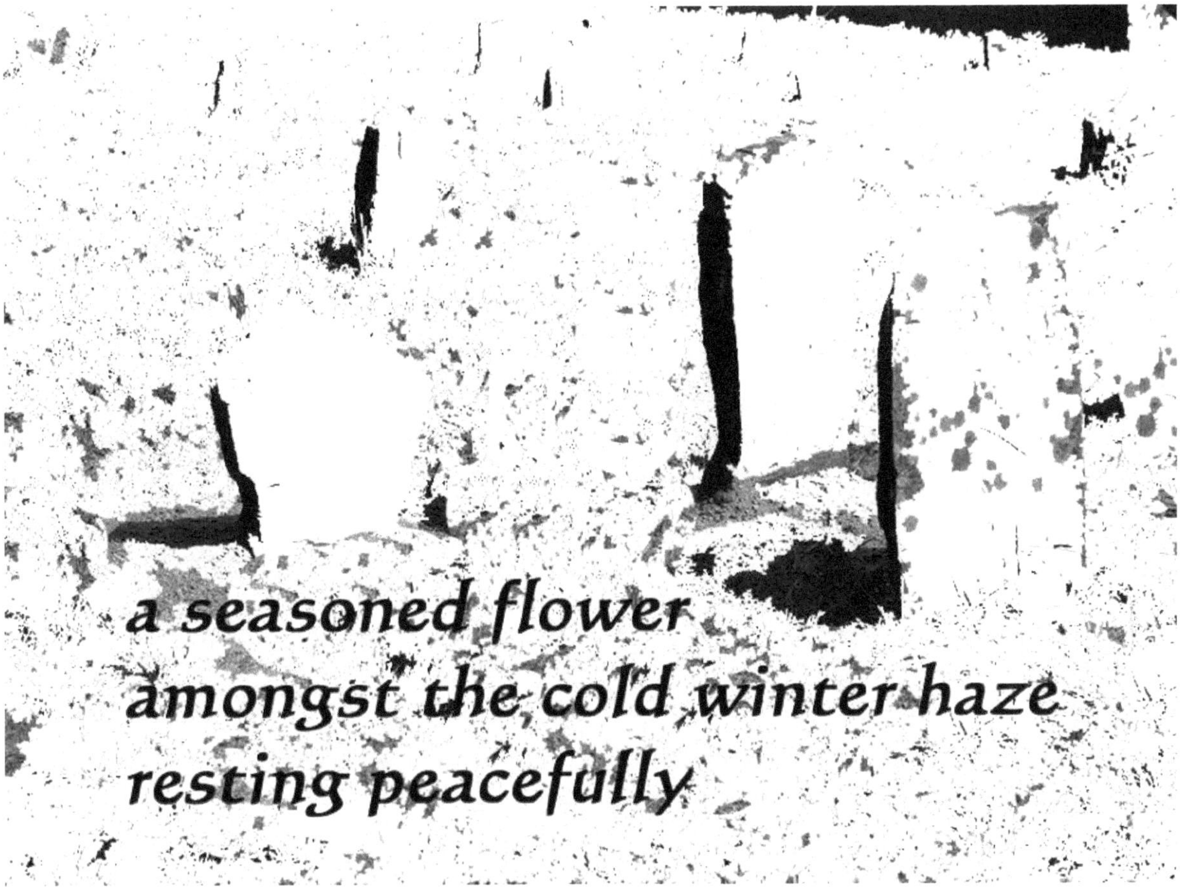


Whitlow, Delbert. 'Revolutionary Soldiers Grave Stones.' Oakvale, Cemetery. Photograph. 2008.

Personal Collection. Kellysville, West Virginia.

Williby-Walker, Debra. 'Daybreak.' Labyrinth on Mama's Knoll, Blanche's Beth Emek.

Photograph. 2014. Personal Collection. Oakvale, West Virginia.

## A Cleansing of my Soul

i walk the winding path
and leisurely sojourn its splendor
one slow step at a time

i walk the winding path
sometimes for solitude
other times for companionship

i walk the winding path
to find my way to focus
i raise my hands in praise

i walk the winding path
God greets me there
through the voices of nature

i walk the winding path
etched out by stones
the labyrinth on the knoll

Williby-Walker, Debra. 'Celebration.' Goodwyn's Chapel. Photograph. 2015.

Personal Collection. Oakvale, West Virginia.

**I am a Refugee**

to flee and bear all and not reveal the pain
the thought lingers

a refugee of my inner circle
with nowhere to escape

exiled from reality
a castoff from others

yet i marvel at my feats
sudden death seems near

only to be rescued
by the one who fails me not

carried away to safety
i fall affectionately at his feet

McCoy-Rodriguez, Rita. 'Moriah's Baptism.' Goodwyn's Chapel Church of Christ, Oakvale, West Virginia. Photograph 2015. Personal Collection. Willowton, West Virginia.

**Transformed**

he came to me…as a dream
visible upon his brow
danced a message of hope

torn by the past…broken
struggling to repair the destruction
declared redemption gauged

existing lifelike relentlessly…a façade
restoration titled by the night
a noble gesture emerged

therapeutic measures considered…within reach
hinged by the burden of sorrow
clemency established; harmoniously redeemed

Williby, Sharon. 'My Serenity.' New River Campground, Narrows, Virginia. Photograph. 2014.

Personal Photograph. Peterstown, West Virginia.

## Casting Above

i may not exist in your presence
…but i live on
take upon your brow
…the soul of my memory
i am the waves crashing against the bank
…your river of song
i am the raging storm
… showering you with my love
take up camp in celebration
…pitch that tent
wade the muddy waters
…embrace the current
i await your arrival
…on the other side
this is not goodbye
…i will throw you a line
find comfort in the ‘Rock’
…the waters are still
my boat has anchored
…in Heaven i fish

Ring. Lisa. 'The Whisper.' Slide Mountain Road. Photograph. 2014. Personal Collection. Bland, Virginia.

## Chosen

the whispers draw me in and i respond to their calling
i follow the faint murmurs but i yearn to understand what is before me
i trudge the valleys and climb the mountains. Why do they lead me?

once lost to the soul of despair, i venture into new territory
the height of my destiny i have yet to reach. i succumb to the voices
one step closer and i tremble with anticipation

the melody of the sound entrances me
i visualize my life with much grace and humbly continue
i am winged forth by a soft breeze as i finish my journey

i see the wonders before me. Why have they chosen me?
the brook fairies

Ring. Lisa. 'Waiting.' Slide Mountain Road. Photograph. 2014. Personal Collection. Bland, Virginia.

## **Guardians**

a weeping soul ceases to awaken to the calling of the night
the night fog settles in and covers the valley with mist
as pixies float beneath the trees of the forest

the wind whispers the secret of the world beyond
much is said in silence gone unnoticed by many
only those with the desire to listen recognizes the agony

silver stars light the way as the one lying motionless rests
tiptoe quietly not to disturb but gently keep watch
dancing occurs in a field of grass undetected

a communal of wee-watchmen carries the message of hope
to the one who waits patiently comfort has emanated
apt findings across the border as go-betweens settle
they are sleeping somewhere near

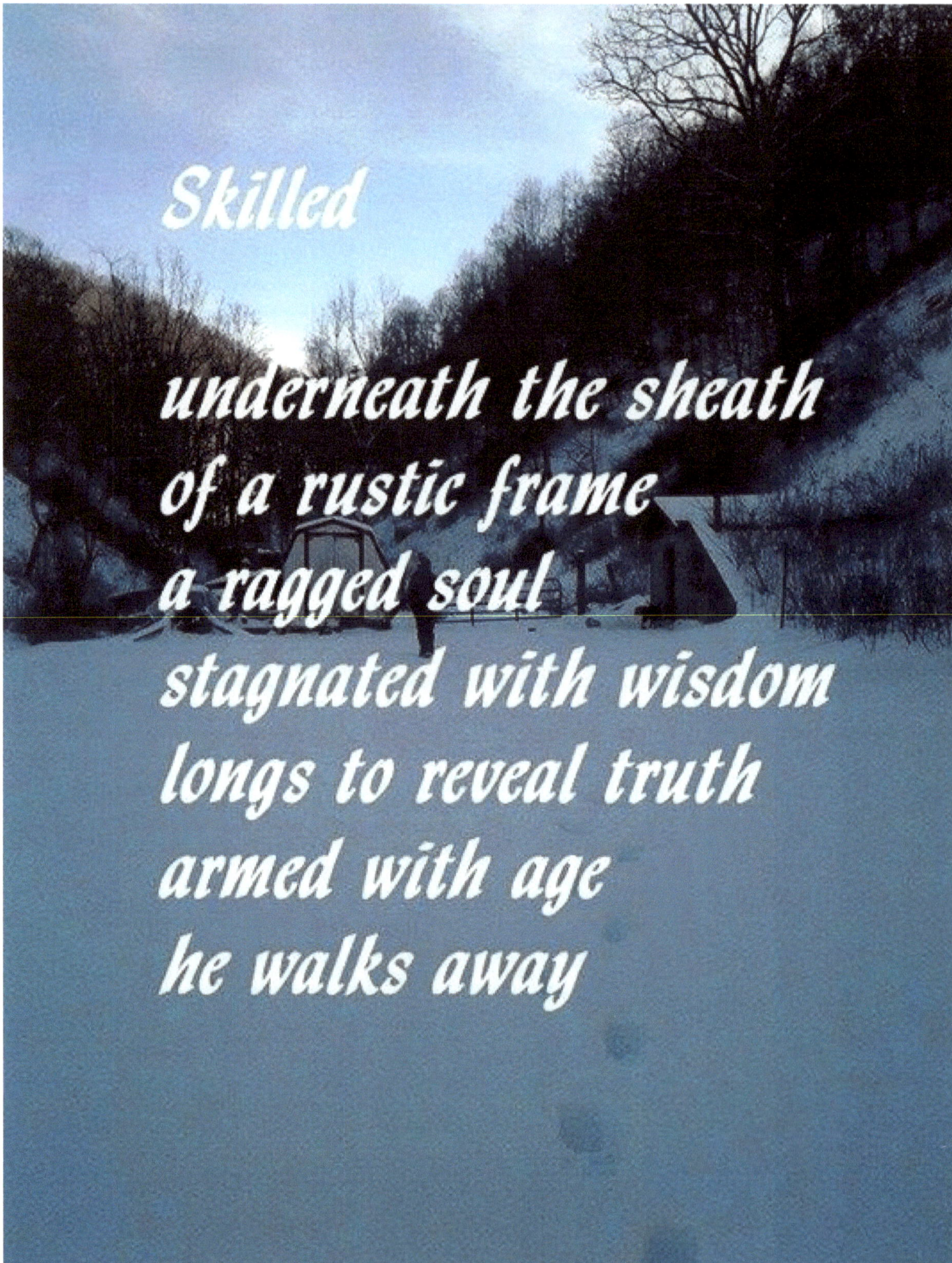


Williby-Walker, Debra. 'Snowstorm 2015.' Blanche's Beth Emek, West Virginia.

Photograph. 2015. Personal Collection, Oakvale, West Virginia.

Sabastian, Lovietta. 'Our Neighbor's Humanity is our Humanity.' Labyrinth Walk at Goodwyn's Chapel.

Photograph. 2014. Personal Collection, Oakvale, West Virginia.

Williby-Walker, Debra. 'Manifestation.' Mama's Knoll, Blanche's Beth Emek.

Photograph. 2015. Personal Collection. Oakvale, West Virginia.

## Enlightened

cold, secluded, and barren
one teardrop from the moon
gave essence to my condition

as the moon-drop fell onto my face
a manifestation evolved
and called my spirit forth

when the wind whistled
and the howling of the wolves
resonated all around me

i fell to my knees
reached for the heavens
and savored the moment within

Byars, Teresa. 'Sunset.' Lester, West Virginia. Photograph. 2014. Personal Collection. Bud, West Virginia.

**Homegoing Through Stages**

in the morning:

the sun rises and all are given life
through His mercy and grace there is hope

during noon:

ignited by the love of Jesus Christ
never-ending love radiates within
each moment grateful for salvation
zealously i seek the path of the Almighty

in the evening:

wisdom i acquired through age and experience
while seeking God's face, i found peace
my heart is healed and mercy received
lift up your spirit and rejoice for me as my time is nigh

during the night:

the sun set and my Father called me home
i am amongst the saints around God's throne

Mills, Savana. 'Forest Floor.' Pencil Sketch on Paper. 2016. Personal Collection, Oakvale, West Virginia.

Burke, Sheila A. 'Base of Uluru.' Uluru, Australia. Photograph. 2013. Personal Collection. West Chester, Pennsylvania.

Walker, LaTisha D. 'The Encounter.' Lewisburg Park. Photograph. 2015.

Personal Collection. Lewisburg, West Virginia.

**A Connection**

in the raging storm
agitated moods take flight
sorrow for them, i feel
as the day carries on
the worries of tomorrow
seize their essence

me? i am exulting
in its beauty and grandeur
i embrace every exquisite
flake, droplet, drizzle, form, rime
each uniquely fashioned in its display
every manifestation of the storm, i snatch

i walk, i hear, i stop, i look, i see
excavation is taking place
i hear the tapping of the billed-drummer
the beating so intense…peck, peck, peck
snowflakes plunder down from the tree
he works, he hears, he stops, he looks, he sees

in that brief moment we connected
…that woodpecker and me

Williby-Walker, Debra. 'Seasons Unite.' Snow Holler. Photograph. 2015.

Personal Collection. Oakvale, West Virginia.

**Seasons Unite**

a summer ray of sunlight discharges its warmth
… betwixt the trees
illuminating a winter snow-iced barren forest floor
…a dirt-covered spot appears
drenched with spring rain and droplets
…nurturing the greenery
a resilient fern guarded by twigs
…a masterpiece
crowned by fall leaves that shield and ensure
…a new birth will ascend

Ring. Lisa. 'Forsaken Memories.' Slide Mountain Road. Photograph. 2014. Personal Collection. Bland, Virginia.

Williby-Walker. Debra. 'Illimination.' Snow Holler. Photograph. 2015.

Personal Collection. Oakvale, West Virginia.

Dunford, Amber. 'La Rosa.' Photograph. 2015. Personal Collection. Guyandotte, Huntington, West Virginia.

**Poetic Beauty**

it came with a touch of dew

..........garden-fresh

the petals resonated

.........an exhibit of unspoken words

each petal designed and shaped with perfection

..........it is only a small rosebud

in it much exposed

...........i hear the silent melody

it sings a song of joy

Redden, Eddie. 'Mystified.' Oil on Cardboard. 2014. Personal Collection. Oakvale, West Virginia.

**Night Light**

bringing light in the darkness
…all powerful with mighty strength

the moon rains down upon
…a shadowed night

beneath the sky, the earth awaits a dawn
…as something magical transpires

the moon rushes in without notice
…a child enchanted by its beauty

a silent connection brings warmth
…to a cold damp night

Williby-Walker, Debra. 'Stream of Stones.' Snow Holler. 2016. Personal Collection, Oakvale, West Virginia.

## She Reigns

consider the follies and woes of a translucent gem
formed by years in the making with each single drip
a polluted underworld trying to block transformation

a jewel breaking free from bondage
she emerges amidst the raging fire
surfaced in beauty she captivates her admirers

the essence of amber

Walker, Moriah B. 'Tower of Stone.' Pinnacle Rock State Park. Photograph.

2015. Personal Collection, Oakvale, West Virginia.

Rain
a part of the life cycle
gently cleansing my soul
droplets of rain

Houghton, Barbara J. 'Imperfection.' Pencil Sketch. 2002. Personal Collection, Oakvale, West Virginia

Ring. Lisa. 'Vangor's Finger.' Slide Mountain Road. Photograph. 2014. Personal Collection. Bland, Virginia.

Chychul, Ellen. 'Mystic Illusion.' Photograph. 2013. Personal Collection. Valleyview, Alberta, Canada.

WIlliby-Walker, Debra. 'Mystic Valley.' Snow Holler. Photograph. 2014. Personal Collection. Oakvale, West Virginia.

Williby-Walker, Debra. 'Sylvan Delight.' Snow Holler. 2015. Photograph.

Personal Collection. Oakvale, West Virginia.

Byars. Teresa. 'Tapered Beauty' Route 54. West Virginia. Photograph. 2014. Personal Collection. Bud, West Virginia.

**Liquefy**

the glistening fairy wands whisper enchantments in the pitch black of night
the desire to be chosen is immense

in sweeps the seeker raging with a sensual glow of hope
the burning flame in his eyes radiate an aspiration to be loved

sexual passion ignites and sparks a state of euphoria
be the glistening fairy wand that melts when chosen

Toussaint, A. M. 'La maison de mauvaise réputation.' Photograph. 2015. Bramwell, West Virginia.

Personal Collection. Princeton, West Virginia.

Burke, Sheila A. 'Betrayal.' Wayland, Massachusetts. Photograph. 2013. Personal Collection. West Chester, Pennsylvania.

Long-Dicey, Sheila. 'Majestic Terrain' Co. Kerry, Ireland. Photograph 2014.

Personal Collection. Harbor City, California.

**You came by way of the river bend; winged**

you came by way of the river bend; winged
the intoxication of your song flowed
with your musings, my heart you stole and ringed
reflected in your eyes and smile, an ode

your kiss precious as the sweet morning dew
my spirit bloomed with the gift of you near
with showers of affection you came through
steaming enchantments seductively dear

alas! a wound on my heart you bequeathed
murderously hurt, many tears trickled
my spirit dampened and troubles seethed
honeyed pleasure maliciously crippled

yet bouquets of memories I recall
the mind-altering fragrance says it all

Long-Dicey. Sheila. 'The Shining.' Sedona, Arizona. Photograph. 2012. Personal Collection. Harbor City, California.

**Forevermore**

what is the essence of your shining? is it to ignite and warm, forevermore?
are your treasures aloft and hidden among the clouds, forevermore?

those rays of light bounce beneath the trees and light my path
ascending down you give me the perception of hope, forevermore

a shadow appears and transcends as a free spirit subject to your presence
you come and go as you perform blissfully among the breezes, forevermore

young innocent beauties seek your warmness and gracefully wait
aggrieved by the transgression, yet you echo your own admirations, forevermore

a thespian in your spirited form of deception and trickery, deb'z is she
i journey in the silence of the darkness----lost----forevermore

Hamm. Tressie. 'A Shade of Melancholy.' Glenwood, West Virginia. Photograph 2012.

Personal Collection, Bluefield, West Virginia.

**Keeper of my Soul**

i am falling amongst the ruin'd
oh sweet doom of natural life
do angels cry when flowers fade?
the way within reach, i believe
come to me great sower of hope

do come through the gate of my heart
rapturously dissolve my tears
end this mayhem of confusion
ascend upon my breast with grace
marked with the delights of passion

hear my silent voice calling you
feed my spirit yearning comfort
pull me from the pits of sadness
come to me, ol' great silver knight
keeper of my soul, i await

Manning, Rae. 'A Weeping.' Pencil Sketch on Paper. 2015. Personal Collection. Morgantown, West Virginia.

**A Weeping**

i fight him
he takes the very breath
of my soul and chokes my spirit

i battle fearlessly
until i am broken by his hold
tears stream down my face

i feel pain
a prisoner trying to break free
my heart aches for comfort

i break the chains
he takes cover within
he hides and waits to resurface

i discover help
through kindred spirits
they understand

Lester, David. 'A Vagabond's Delight.' Kelly's Tank. 2013. Personal Collection, Princeton, West Virginia.

## The Journey

the grand entrance is but a fleeting moment
many feats are won but scars remain
combat wounds ravage the soul
the few inklings of hope meander
waiting for an exit

Mills. Savana. 'The Soul.' Pencil Sketch. 2015. Personal Collection. Oakvale, West Virginia.

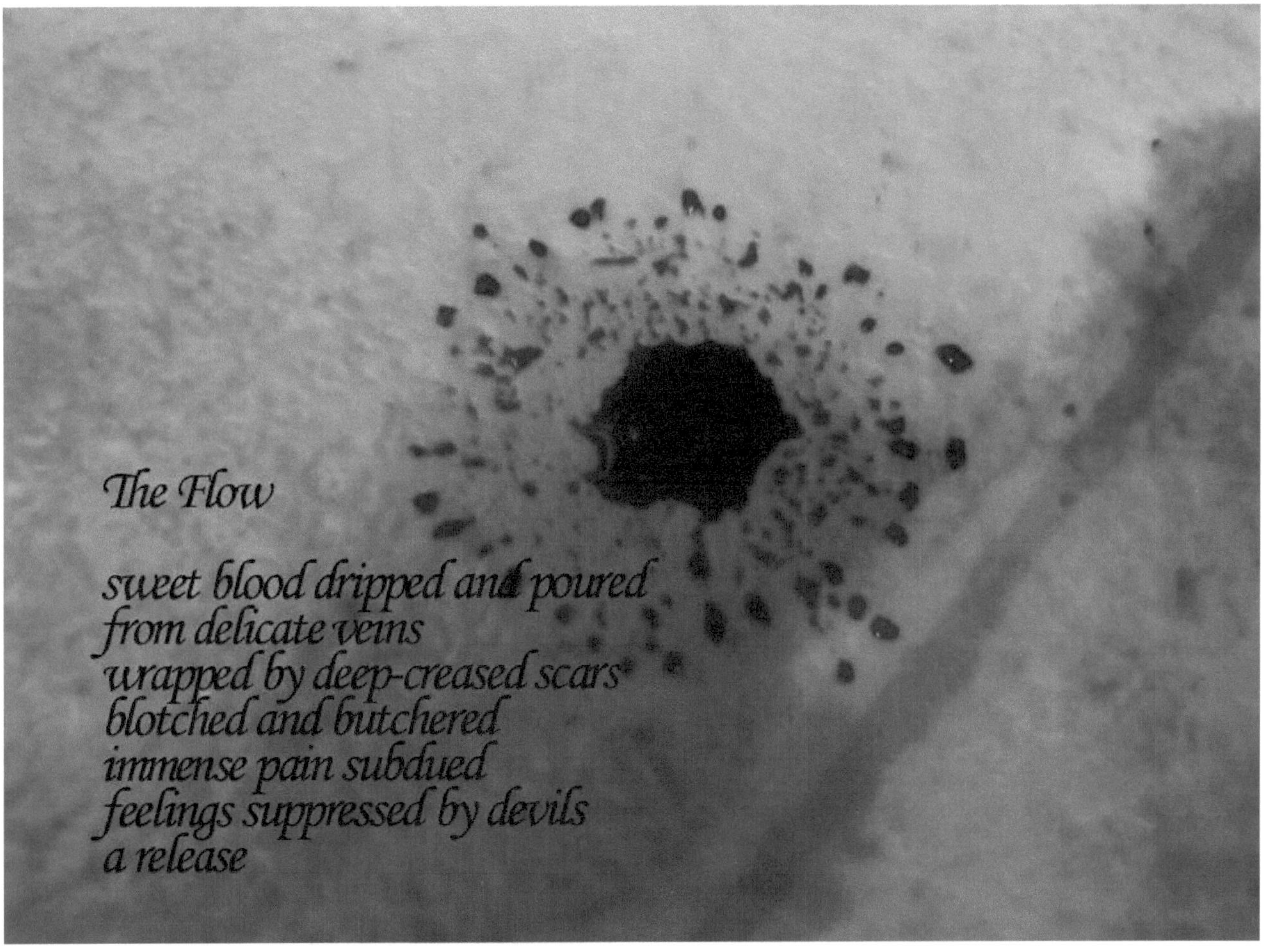


Chychul. Ellen 'Crimson Drop.' Photograph. 2012. Personal Collection. Valleyview, Alberta, Canada.

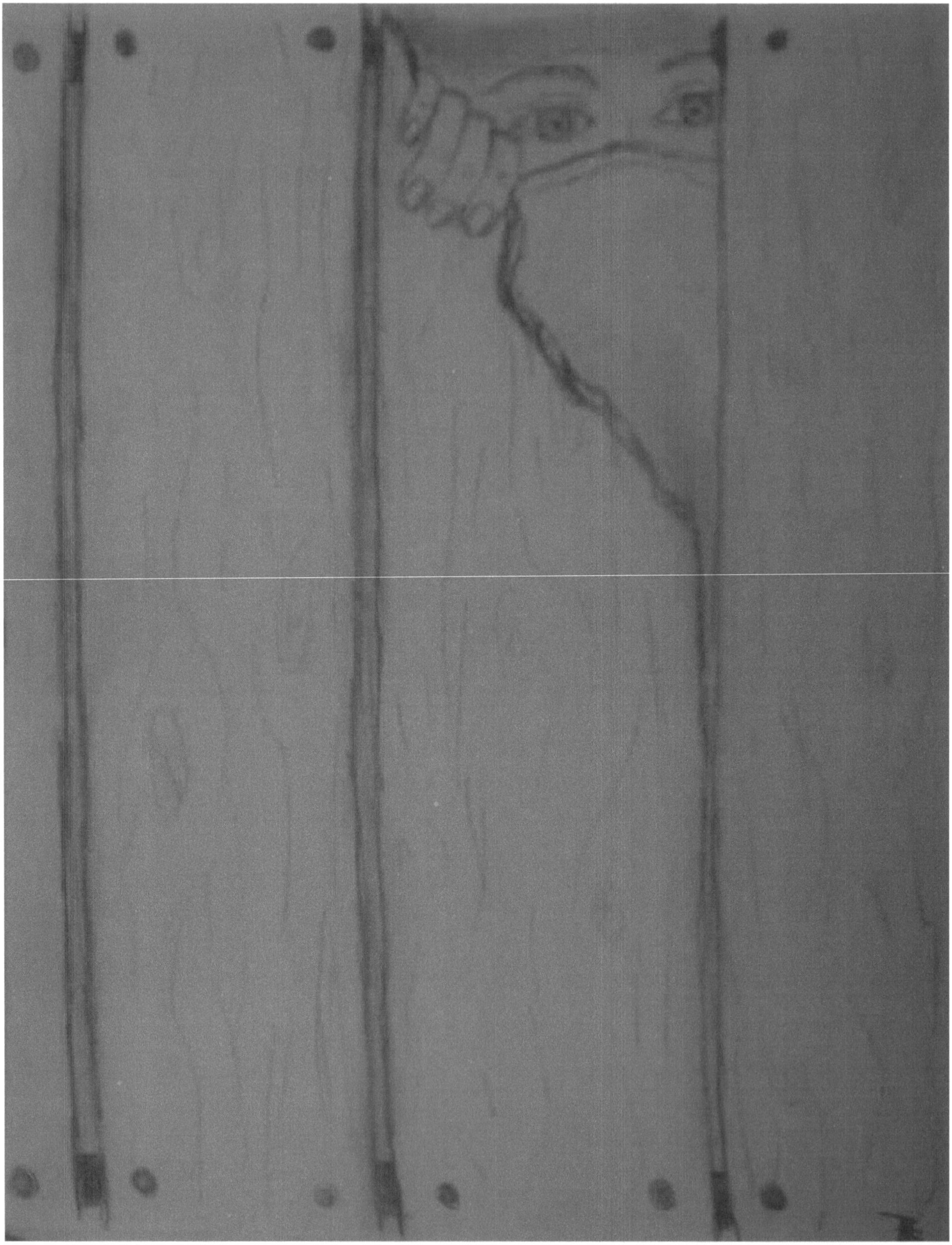

Houghton, Barbara J. 'Solitary.' Pencil Sketch on Paper.' 2015. Personal Collection. Mercer County, West Virginia.

**Beneath the Veil**

in the stillness
visions appear often
she sees

in the night
within her dreams
she soars

in the moonlight
iniquity is atoned
she breathes

in the darkness
beneath the veil
she lives

Toussaint, A. M. 'La Maison D'Antan.' Photograph. 2015. Bramwell, West Virginia.

Personal Collection. Princeton, West Virginia.

**The Chamber**

empty, cold, majestic, all alone
a dwelling from a time long past
...inside the frame, it stirs

empty, cold, majestic, all alone
memories scattered inside
...aged and battered, it cries

empty, cold, majestic, all alone
flawed reality within
...blistered and tainted, it wails

empty, cold, majestic, all alone
marked with a sense of pride
...beaten and weathered, it sighs

empty, cold, majestic, all alone
it waves to the passerby
...soon to be forgotten, it dies

Walker. Marcus D. 'West Virginia State Penitentiary, Gothic Style Prison. 1992.

Personal Collection. Oakvale, West Virginia.

**Taken**

dawn brings no sunshine to unveil the mourning of the night
shackled by the nightmare of the macabre is so monstrous to the soul
the rigorous strike is an arrow piercing the heart endlessly

visions of the apparition shake the center like an earthquake to devour the weak
...taken to a chasm cold as a blistering winter steeped with ungodliness
marked by the cage where one is faced with an abrupt convexity

the strategy is endless as the walls reveal their secrets of survival
written words release an escape likened to the wingspan of an eagle, free
...conversations bleed joyful sorrow and the voice echoes an appreciated love

laughter is sacred and each second is precious gold filtered through the wire
conformation of sanity and security of the restrained sensed, two prisoners...
a son deep in the pits of the underworld and a mother held captive by the torment

Manning, Rae. 'Terror Within.' Charcoal on Paper. 2015. Personal Collection. Morgantown, West Virginia.

**Terror Within**

as the night sky darkens and the moon barely peeks through the clouds
i am drawn into the depths of the unknown visualizing the evil spirit that enslaves my soul
i seek comfort from my defenders but none are to be found

…only the stillness befriends me
my accusers stand crouched beneath the trees
…and curse my very existence with detestation

i am broken and branded by torment and torture
only the dawn in my dreams capture my desire to be free
a prisoner of my own imagination cultivated by the demon of the night

Williby-Walker, Debra. 'Serene Agitation.' 2013. Blanche's Beth Emek.

Personal Collection. Oakvale, West Virginia.

Williby-Walker, Debra. 'Desolation.' Blanche's Beth Emek. Photograph. 2012.

Personal Collection. Oakvale, West Virginia.

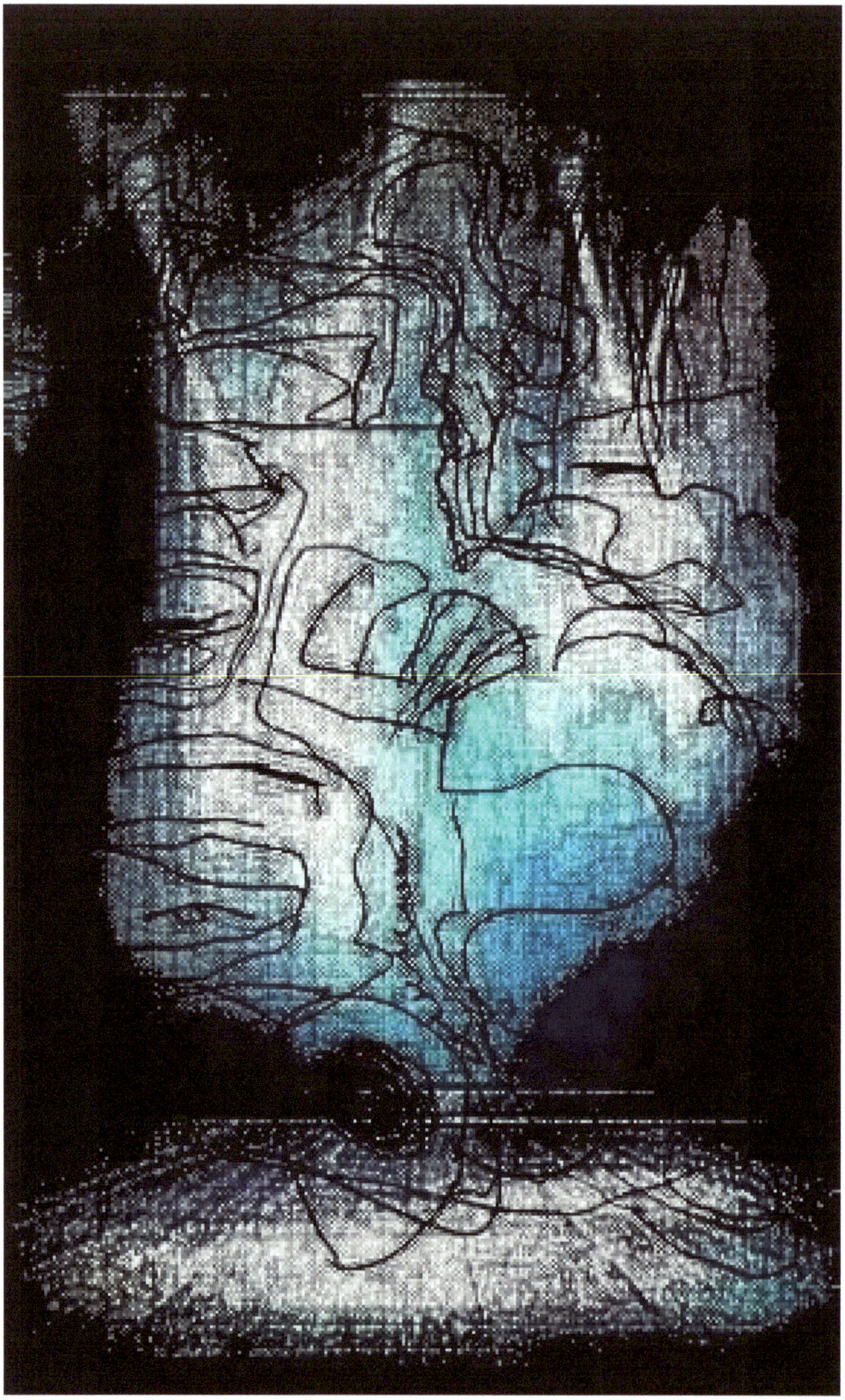

Walker, Braydin Michael-Andrew. (Brady). 'Webbed Thoughts.' Ink Sketch on Paper Enhanced with Graphic Art.

2015. Personal Collection, Blanche's Beth Emek, Oakvale, West Virginia.

**Poetry Unleashed**

the spirit of the mind
is lost in a maze of madness

uncontrollable and painful
at times, the pace is too much

mental genius takes place
through racing thoughts

in the quest to seek control
evolves a creation of verse

**Verse Inspiration**

A Seasoned Flower in memory of Nancy Williby pg. 19

Casting Above in memory of Robert (Bobby) Darrell Williby pg. 27

Homegoing Through Stages in memory of Inez French pg. 37

~

She Reigns dedicated to my friend Amber Dunford! May this gem always emerge amidst the raging fire. Pg. 51

Publisher: Debra June Williby-Walker

www.ingramcontent.com/pod-product-compliance
Lightning Source LLC
Chambersburg PA
CBHW042001150426
43194CB00002B/83
* 9 7 8 0 6 9 2 7 0 2 9 1 8 *